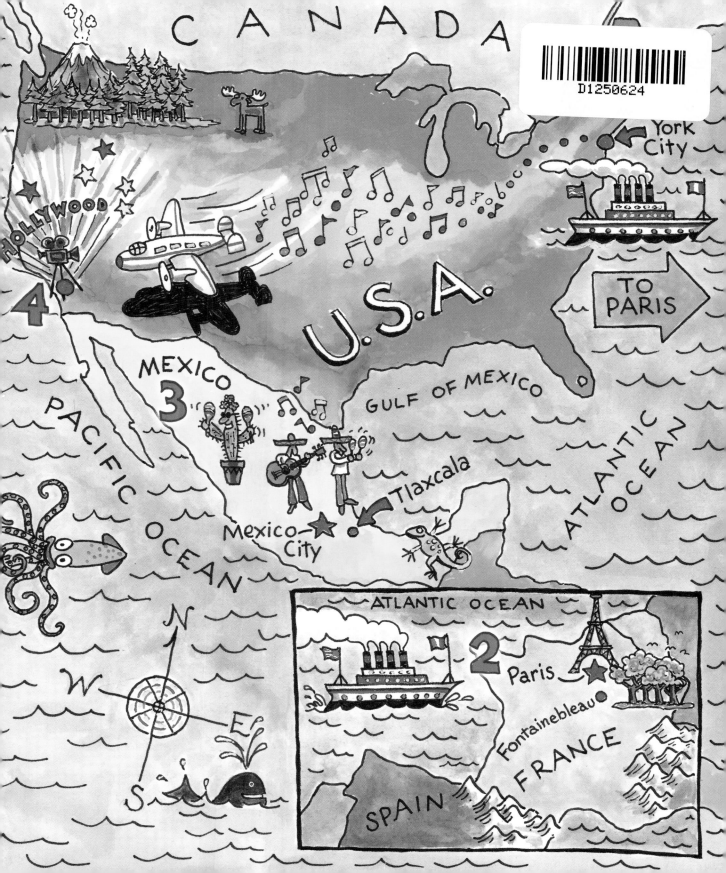

TIMELINE OF AARON COPLAND'S LIFE

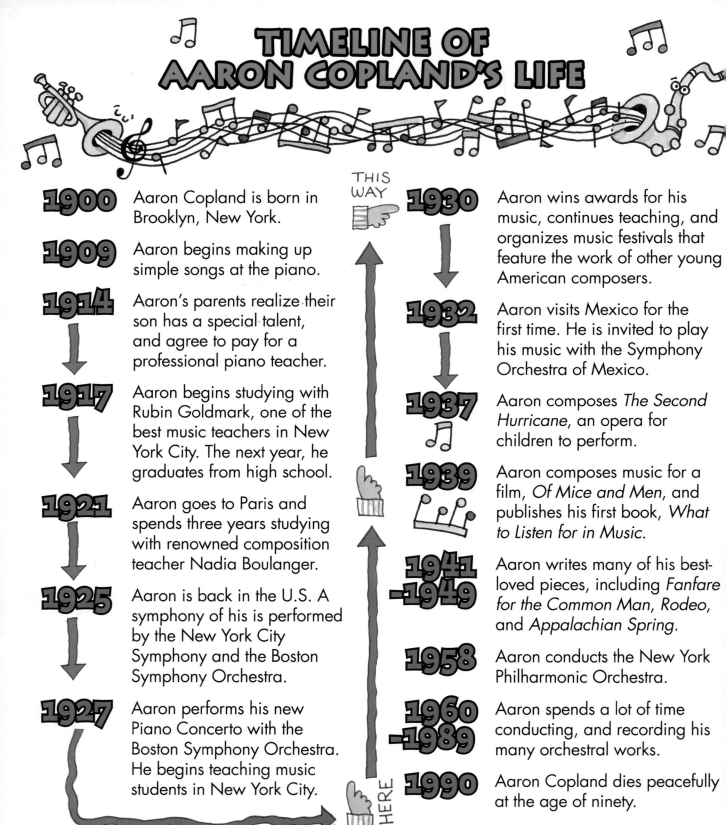

THIS WAY

1900 Aaron Copland is born in Brooklyn, New York.

1909 Aaron begins making up simple songs at the piano.

1914 Aaron's parents realize their son has a special talent, and agree to pay for a professional piano teacher.

1917 Aaron begins studying with Rubin Goldmark, one of the best music teachers in New York City. The next year, he graduates from high school.

1921 Aaron goes to Paris and spends three years studying with renowned composition teacher Nadia Boulanger.

1925 Aaron is back in the U.S. A symphony of his is performed by the New York City Symphony and the Boston Symphony Orchestra.

1927 Aaron performs his new Piano Concerto with the Boston Symphony Orchestra. He begins teaching music students in New York City.

UP HERE

1930 Aaron wins awards for his music, continues teaching, and organizes music festivals that feature the work of other young American composers.

1932 Aaron visits Mexico for the first time. He is invited to play his music with the Symphony Orchestra of Mexico.

1937 Aaron composes *The Second Hurricane*, an opera for children to perform.

1939 Aaron composes music for a film, *Of Mice and Men*, and publishes his first book, *What to Listen for in Music*.

1941 -1949 Aaron writes many of his best-loved pieces, including *Fanfare for the Common Man*, *Rodeo*, and *Appalachian Spring*.

1958 Aaron conducts the New York Philharmonic Orchestra.

1960 -1989 Aaron spends a lot of time conducting, and recording his many orchestral works.

1990 Aaron Copland dies peacefully at the age of ninety.

GETTING TO KNOW
THE WORLD'S
GREATEST COMPOSERS

A A R O N
COPLAND

WRITTEN AND ILLUSTRATED BY MIKE VENEZIA

CONSULTANT
DONALD FREUND, PROFESSOR OF COMPOSITION,
INDIANA UNIVERSITY SCHOOL OF MUSIC

CHILDREN'S PRESS®

An Imprint of Scholastic Inc.

For my parents, Eugene and Patricia Venezia

Picture Acknowledgements
Photographs ©: cover and title page: Stock Montage; 3: AP Images; 10: Aaron Copland Collection/ Library of Congress; 13 top: Bequest of Dorothea Dreier to the Collection Société Anonyme/Yale University Art Gallery; 13 bottom: Purchased with funds from the Coffin Fine Arts Trust, Nathan Emory Coffin Collection of the Des Moines Art Center, 1962.21; 14: Time Life Pictures/ Getty Images; 15 left: Stock Montage/Superstock, Inc.; 15 right: AP Images; 16: Al Fenn/Getty Images; 17: Musée des Arts Decoratifs, Paris, France/Erich Lessing/Art Resource, NY; 18-19: *Blues*, 1929 (oil on canvas), Motley Jr., Archibald J. (1891-1981)/Private Collection/© Valerie Gerrard Browne/Chicago History Museum/Bridgeman Images; 20: Richard Tucker/Getty Images; 24: © 2018 Museum Associates/LACMA, licensed by Art Resource, NY and © 2018 Banco de México Diego Rivera Frida Kahlo Museums Trust, Mexico, D.F./Artists Rights Society (ARS), New York; 26: Print Collector/Getty Images; 27: Publicity photograph of Christina Johnson and Eddie Shellman for the dance production Billy the Kid/Martha Swope/New York Public Library; 29: Thomas Hart Benton, American, 1889–1975; *Cradling Wheat*, 1938; tempera and oil on board; 31 1/4 x 39 1/4 inches; Saint Louis Art Museum, Museum Purchase 8:1939; 30 top: Mary Altaffer/AP Images; 30 bottom: Constance Bannister Corp/Getty Images; 31 top: Culver Pictures; 31 bottom: Martell/AP Images; 32: Stock Montage.

Library of Congress Cataloging-in-Publication Data

Names: Venezia, Mike, author, illustrator.
Title: Aaron Copland / written and illustrated by Mike Venezia; consultant, Donald Freund.
Description: Revised edition. | New York, NY : Children's Press, 2018. | Series: Getting to know the world's greatest composers | Includes bibliographical references and index.
Identifiers: LCCN 2017048074| ISBN 9780531228678 (library binding) | ISBN 9780531233702 (pbk.)
Subjects: LCSH: Copland, Aaron, 1900-1990--Juvenile literature. | Composers--United States--Biography--Juvenile literature.
Classification: LCC ML3930.C66 V4 2018 | DDC 780.92 [B] --dc23 LC record available at https://lccn.loc.gov/2017048074

Scholastic Inc., 557 Broadway, New York, NY 10012.

1 2 3 4 5 6 7 8 9 10 R 27 26 25 24 23 22 21 20 19 18

Aaron Copland in 1956

Aaron Copland was one of America's greatest composers. He was born in 1900, right at the beginning of a new century and the age of modern times. Aaron not only loved to write music—he also loved teaching people how to enjoy it.

Aaron Copland's best-known music sounds crisp and clear and simple. It often gives you a feeling of being out West at an exciting rodeo, or in wide-open spaces, or in a peaceful countryside. Some people have a hard time figuring out how Aaron Copland

was able to write music like this, since he spent most of his life in a big city. Aaron didn't think it was necessary to live in the places he wrote music about. With his great imagination, he could just about picture himself being there.

Aaron grew up in busy Brooklyn, New York. He had two older brothers and two older sisters. His parents owned a big department store. The whole family helped out there.

Even when he was very young, Aaron helped out by working as a salesman in the toy department.

Aaron Copland started showing an interest in music when he was about seven years old. He spent hours listening to records on his cousin's phonograph, which was a new invention at that time.

    Aaron also started pestering his sister Laurine whenever she practiced the piano. He finally got her to give him some lessons. Aaron started to make up his own songs right away. When he was a teenager, he persuaded his parents to send him to a "real" teacher.

Aaron's parents, Harris and Sarah Copland, in front of their store in 1922

Mr. and Mrs. Copland agreed to pay for Aaron's lessons as long as he found his own teacher. The Coplands thought it was important to give their children responsibility and the best opportunities they could.

Both of Aaron's parents had come to America from Russia at a time when many people in Russia were homeless and had no money. Aaron's father often reminded his children of what a great country the United States was, and how lucky they were to be there.

Aaron always remembered what his father said, especially when he began to write his most famous music.

At the beginning of the twentieth century, when Aaron Copland was growing up, people in America were just getting used to modern life. There were all kinds of modern inventions popping up.

Battle of Lights, Coney Island, Mardi Gras,
by Joseph Stella, 1913

Artists and writers were trying out modern ideas, too. It seemed like everything was becoming new and exciting—everything except America's classical music.

Abstraction on Spectrum (Organization 5), by Stanton MacDonald Wright, ca. 1914–17

Classical music lovers in America seemed
satisfied listening to music that had been
written years before by great European
composers like Mozart, Beethoven, and Chopin.

So, Beethoven,
Chopin,
what's new?

Austrian composer
Wolfgang Amadeus
Mozart (1756–1791)

German composer Ludwig
van Beethoven (1770–1827)

Polish composer Frédéric
Chopin (1810–1849)

Aaron learned about and respected these
composers, but he felt it was important to
learn about American music and modern
composers, too.

Nadia Boulanger

When Aaron was twenty years old, he got a chance to study music in Paris, France. Paris was the modern-music center of the world. Aaron's teacher was Nadia Boulanger, one of the best composition teachers of the twentieth century.

Watercolor sketch of a set design for Maurice Ravel's ballet
Daphnis and Chloe, by Leon Bakst, 1912

Many of her students went on to become famous composers. Aaron was very excited. He started learning about modern composers, like Igor Stravinsky and Maurice Ravel. These composers weren't afraid to try new and different things. They often shocked people with musical sounds that had never been heard before.

While he was studying in Paris, Aaron sometimes took time off and traveled with his friends to different countries. On one trip, Aaron noticed that wherever he went, bands were playing a lively kind of music that had been invented by African American musicians. It was called jazz. Even though jazz had originated in America, it was becoming very popular in Europe. Since Aaron was interested in writing American-sounding music, he thought it might be a good idea to add some jazz sounds to the modern classical music he was starting to write.

Blues, by Archibald John Motley, Jr., 1929

Serge Koussevitzky

The music Aaron came up with was very original. Nadia Boulanger liked it a lot and asked Aaron to play it for some of her important friends. One of those friends was Serge Koussevitzky, the new music conductor of the Boston Symphony Orchestra. Mr. Koussevitzky liked Aaron's music, too, and agreed to play one of his new pieces at a concert.

When Aaron's *Symphony for Organ and Orchestra* was played, a lot of people didn't like it. Some of them even booed!

They probably didn't care for the modern sound, especially the jazzy parts. At the time, Aaron Copland didn't really mind if people disliked his music. He knew it might take a while for people to get used to it, because it sounded so different from music they had heard before.

Aaron kept adding jazz rhythms, and experimented with other sounds to make his music as original and modern as possible. For a while, his music became more and more complicated. Sometimes, even musicians in the orchestra found it almost too hard to play. Aaron started to notice that only people who were very serious about music were able to understand and appreciate his new music. This wasn't what he wanted at all. Aaron Copland wanted everyone in America to be able to enjoy his music.

Baile en Tehuantepec,
by Diego Rivera, ca. 1935

Right around this time, Aaron got a
chance to visit Mexico. He noticed that
music was much more a part of people's lives
in Mexico than it was in the United States.

Aaron heard people playing guitars and singing, and saw people dancing wherever he went. Once, when he went to a large dance hall, Aaron became so excited by the joyful, fast-moving music being played that he decided to write a music piece about Mexico. Aaron took bits and pieces of Mexican folk tunes, and put them together with his own music. Aaron called his new piece *El Salón México*. When you listen to it, it's easy to imagine the people and beautiful countryside of Mexico.

W hen *El Salón México* was played, it gave people a happy feeling. The piece soon became very popular. Aaron realized that he was on the right track to writing music that more people could enjoy.

In 1939, Aaron was asked to write some music for a ballet about the legendary Wild West outlaw Billy the Kid.

William H. Bonney, alias Billy the Kid

A scene from Aaron Copland's ballet *Billy the Kid* as performed by the Dance Theatre of Harlem

Aaron had always loved stories about the Old West. He thought he would write *Billy the Kid* in the same way that he had written *El Salón México*. But instead of using parts of Mexican folk songs, Aaron used American folk songs in his piece.

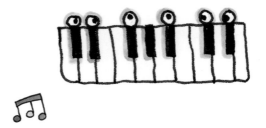

In *Billy the Kid*, you can hear familiar folk songs here and there, like "Git Along Little Dogies" and "Bury Me Not on the Lone Prairie." People liked hearing parts of songs they had known while they were growing up. At that time, people in America were worried. It was the Great Depression, when many Americans lost their jobs and savings and became poor. It also looked like the United States was about to get into a serious war that had already started in Europe.

Cradling Wheat, by Thomas Hart Benton, 1938

Artists, writers, and composers began looking around at the everyday things that made America great. They put what they saw and heard into paintings, books, and music. Their works gave people a feeling of comfort and hope, and helped make them proud of their country.

A scene from *Appalachian Spring*, as performed by the Martha Graham Dance Company

Aaron Copland went on to compose many famous pieces, including *Fanfare for the Common Man* (part of his Third Symphony) and the ballets *Rodeo* and *Appalachian Spring*. Even though he used parts of American cowboy, riverboat, and railroad songs, Aaron combined them with his own music to come up with a very special, exciting, and beautiful all-American sound.

A scene from *Rodeo*, as performed by Agnes de Mille and Frederic Franklin in New York City in 1942

Aaron also went to Hollywood for a while and wrote some music for movies. He even won an Academy Award for the music he wrote for a movie called *The Heiress.*

Aaron Copland lived to be ninety years old. As he grew older, he spent less time writing and more time conducting music and teaching. Aaron Copland told his students to always be original, to experiment with their music, and to make music that was part of modern times.

Aaron Copland conducting a rehearsal of the Boston Symphony Orchestra in 1980

Aaron Copland with one of his students

Although Aaron Copland was very busy throughout his life, he always found time to help out young composers. He worked hard to put on concerts so that many people could learn to enjoy music. He also wrote music that was just for high-school students to play in their bands and orchestras.

Today, Aaron Copland's music is as popular as ever, so it's easy to find it online for free. You can also probably borrow recordings from your local library.

LEARN MORE BY TAKING THE COPLAND QUIZ!

(ANSWERS ON THE NEXT PAGE.)

1. Aaron Copland wrote exciting western-style music even though he lived in big cities for most of his life. He was always good at finding ways to get himself in a cowboy-music-writing mood. What was one thing that helped him?
  a He took horseback-riding lessons in Central Park.
  b He invited Annie Oakley to his house for dinner every week.
  c He remembered cowboy movies he had seen as a kid.

2. One of Copland's best-loved works is *A Lincoln Portrait*, in which music accompanies a person reading Abe Lincoln's best speeches. Many famous people have narrated Lincoln's words. Aaron's all-time favorite reader, though, was Carl Sandburg. Who was Carl Sandburg?
  a The actor who provides the voice of Homer Simpson
  b One of America's greatest poets and authors
  c Abe Lincoln's great-grandson

3. Aaron Copland loved pets and always had a dog or cat around the house. He once named a Great Dane after his favorite music teacher. What was his pet dog's name?
  a Igor Stravinsky
  b Duke Ellington
  c Nadia Boulanger

4. Why did Aaron Copland, one of America's greatest composers, pretty much stop writing music when he got older?
  a He got tired of listening to his neighbors complain about his piano practicing.
  b He just ran out of ideas.
  c He was satisfied just listening to his music on the radio.

5. Copland is the only American *classical* music composer to be honored by having…
  a His home made into a National Historic Landmark
  b A 60-foot image of his head carved on Mount Rushmore
  c An aircraft carrier named after him

ANSWERS

1. **c** Aaron recalled cowboy movies he had seen as a kid growing up in Brooklyn. Aaron didn't think it was unusual for him, or any kid, to get a feeling of the old West by watching an exciting movie that featured one of his favorite cowboy-movie heroes of the day.

2. **b** Carl Sandburg was an American poet and writer. He was a good choice to read along with Aaron Copland's music. Sandburg was an expert on Abraham Lincoln. One of his greatest works is a six-volume book about Abe Lincoln's life.

3. **c** Aaron Copland met Nadia Boulanger when he was a student in France. He said he believed there wasn't a thing she didn't know about music. Nadia introduced Aaron to many of the best composers and conductors of the day. Most importantly, she knew how to teach and inspire her students to be the best composers and musicians they could be.

4. **b** As he got older, Aaron composed less and less. He said it was as if one day, someone had simply turned off his idea faucet! Aaron kept super-busy, though, for the rest of his life. He traveled, conducted orchestras, taught, and recorded his music.

5. **a** Aaron would often get away from the busy city to work in the peaceful countryside of New York State. He decided to buy a house in Cortlandt Manor, just north of New York City. Today, the Copland House is a National Historic Landmark. American composers who are approved can live there free for a month or two while they work on their music.